SUPER SMART INFORMATION STRATEGIES

INFORMATION EXPLORER

FIND THE RIGHT SITE

by Ann Truesdell

CHERRY LAKE PUBLISHING • ANN ARBOR, MICHIGAN

CHERRY LAKE
Publishing

Published in the United States of America
by Cherry Lake Publishing
Ann Arbor, Michigan
www.cherrylakepublishing.com

Content Adviser: Gail Dickinson, PhD,
Associate Professor, Old Dominion University,
Norfolk, Virginia

Book design and illustration: The Design Lab

Photo credits: Cover, ©iStockphoto.com/vgajic; pages 3, 11, 22, and 29
bottom, ©iStockphoto.com/bluestocking; page 8, ©Sensay, used under
license from Shutterstock, Inc.; pages 16, 24, and 29 top, ©Jazza, used
under license from Shutterstock, Inc.; page 20, ©WoodyStock/Alamy; page
23, ©Jacek Chabraszewski, used under license from Shutterstock, Inc.;
page 26, ©Pablo Paul/Alamy

Library of Congress Cataloging-in-Publication Data
Truesdell, Ann.
Super smart information strategies. Find the right site / by Ann
Truesdell.
      p. cm.—(Information explorer)
   Includes bibliographical references and index.
   ISBN-13: 978-1-60279-638-6   ISBN-10: 1-60279-638-6 (lib. bdg.)
   ISBN-13: 978-1-60279-646-1   ISBN-10: 1-60279-646-7 (pbk.)
   1. Computer network resources—Evaluation—Juvenile literature. I. Title.
II. Series.
   ZA4201.T78 2010
   025.042—dc22
                                                            2009027083

Cherry Lake Publishing would like to acknowledge the work
of The Partnership for 21st Century Skills. Please visit
www.21stcenturyskills.org for more information.

Printed in the United States of America
Corporate Graphics Inc.
January 2010
CLSP06

A NOTE TO PARENTS
AND TEACHERS: Please
remind your children
how to stay safe online
before they do the
activities in this book.

A NOTE TO KIDS:
Always remember
your safety comes
first!

Table of Contents

Chapter One
4 **Are These Facts Correct?**

Chapter Two
13 **Who Wrote This Stuff?**

Chapter Three
17 **Why Is This Web Site Here?**

Chapter Four
21 **Judging a ~~Book~~ Web Site by Its Cover**

Chapter Five
25 **Putting the Clues Together**

30 Glossary
31 Find Out More
32 Index
32 About the Author

CHAPTER ONE

Are These Facts Correct?

"I expect to be impressed," your teacher says after explaining your assignment. Your project: write a history report. Your topic: the life of Christopher Columbus. So you head to the school library. After sitting at a computer station, you get to work. You do a Google search by typing "Columbus" in the search window. Your search returns millions of results. Some are about Christopher Columbus. But some are about the city of Columbus, Ohio. You choose the first one titled "Christopher Columbus." You jot down the information you found from that site.

Christopher Columbus and Columbus, Ohio, are two very different topics!

4

Take a close look at a Web site before deciding if it's right for your information need.

Finding the perfect site for your project, however, is not that easy. Smart researchers make sure they've found good Web sites. What makes a Web site valuable? Good sites have accurate information. They are also up-to-date. What else makes a site right for your needs? We'll find out through the process of Web site evaluation.

Web site evaluation involves taking a close look at a Web site. Your goal is to decide if the Web site is right for your research. The process is a bit like detective work. You are investigating the Web site to see if its information is correct. It's important to know where your information comes from and who put it there.

You should find out who the author of the Web site is. Decide if you want to trust that person to give you information.

Try to determine if the site was meant for students, specifically students your age. Is the page made up completely of text? Is the vocabulary or reading level very advanced? Does the site express a single point of view? If so, the site is probably meant for older researchers. Sites designed for students often help you learn about something. Their purpose is to inform. The best are developed by experts or organizations related to the topic.

Some web sites are created with kids in mind.

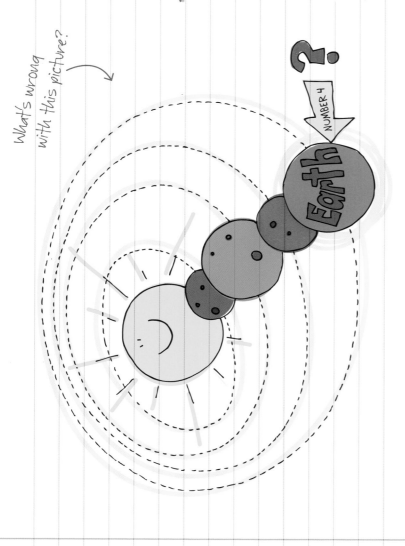

What's wrong with this picture?

NUMBER 4

Earth

Once you find a Web site on your topic, make sure the information it contains is accurate. You will have to read through a bit of the text on the page. Based on what you already know about the topic, does the information make sense? Let's say you are doing a project about Earth. The site says that Earth is the fourth planet from the sun. Stop right there! That is a big error. You cannot trust the information on this site. Move on with your search. At this stage, you are determining how to act on the information that you come across. You will keep the accurate Web sites. You will reject the others. And you will modify your search terms if you cannot find what you are looking for.

Web sites are just one source of information. You will use books for research projects, too.

Next, dig a little deeper. Check a Web site's information against data from a source that you know you can trust. These include encyclopedias, textbooks, or Web sites recommended by your teacher or librarian. You should also try using more than one Web site for your project. Compare facts from one Web site to facts presented in two different sites. Does the information agree?

Another clue you should look for is the date that the Web site was created. You should also check when the Web site was last updated. Information changes over time. You will want to find sites that have been updated in the last 5 years for research on history

8

topics. For current events, you want to find sites that have been updated this year.

Think about the site's purpose, too. This is the reason that the Web site exists in the first place. Some sites are created because a company wishes to sell a product. Other sites exist because the author wants to persuade you to believe something. If you are researching a topic such as Christopher Columbus, you will want a Web site that exists to inform. Informational sites are meant to teach and present the facts. Their goal is not to sell something or persuade you. They are not biased. That means they do not intend to make you favor only one point of view or think a certain way.

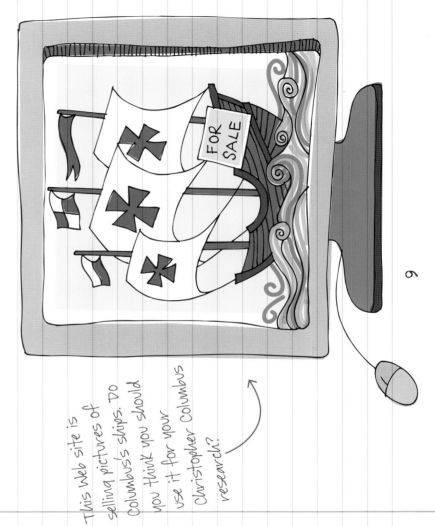

This Web site is selling pictures of Columbus's ships. Do you think you should use it for your Christopher Columbus research?

Finally, you will often want to find a site that lists references. References are the books, articles, or Web sites that the site author used to get his or her information. These references are sometimes found in a section of the site titled "Bibliography" or "Works Cited." In this section, you may also find links to other sites that you can use for your report. A list of references can show you that the author of the site worked hard to find accurate information.

Did you Know this?

If you choose to explore the Web sites given as examples in this book, be sure to type the Web addresses exactly as they appear in the text. If you miss even one character, type the address exactly as it appears and that particular page has been updated or deleted. Try going to the site's home page and searching for the information.

TRY THIS!

It's time to practice judging if a site has accurate information. Compare two sites about Christopher Columbus. Here are two possible options:

Site A:

www.allaboutexplorers.com/explorers/columbus.html

Site B:

www.bbc.co.uk/schools/famouspeople/standard/columbus/index.shtml

Follow these steps as you examine the web sites:

1. Read through the information on Site A. Does it seem accurate to you? Why or why not?

2. Read through Site B. Does this data seem accurate? Why or why not?

3. Ask a librarian or teacher to help you find an encyclopedia article on Columbus. Compare the information in that article to the information on both sites. Does all the information agree?

(continued on page 12)

When reading information on a web site, ask yourself whether what you are reading is true. Just because it is on the web site, doesn't mean it is a true statement.

11

TRY THIS! (CONTINUED)

Which site is a better source of accurate information? Which clues helped you make that decision? Hopefully, you chose Site B. By skimming the text on Site A, you should have noticed that many details were incorrect. Maybe you weren't sure. But comparing those details to the information in the encyclopedia article probably helped you be certain. Also, Site B is sponsored by the BBC, which is the British Broadcasting Corporation. One of its main goals is to educate and inform. Knowing a bit about the BBC would probably help you decide that you can trust the information on its site. With practice, you'll get better at evaluating the accuracy of the sites you find online.

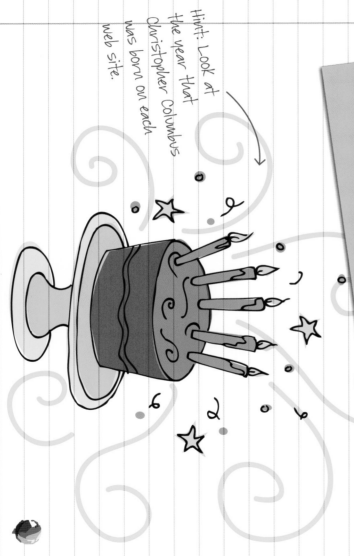

Hint: Look at the year that Christopher Columbus was born on each web site.

12

CHAPTER TWO

Who Wrote This Stuff?

So you've skimmed a Web site. You've checked some facts against reliable sources. Now you can trust the information on the site, right? Not so fast! The next step in your detective work is to find out who is the author of the Web site. The clues you find about the author can help you decide if the information is accurate. The best Web site authors are experts on the topic you are researching. Experts are people who know a lot about a topic, skill, or thing. Experts have a lot of experience. They often have advanced educational degrees.

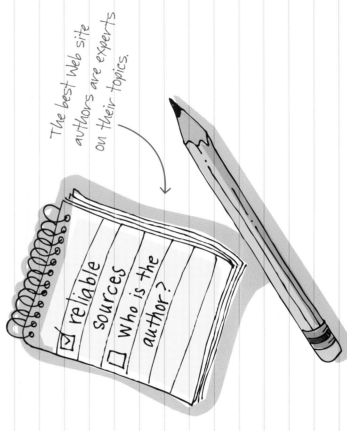

The best Web site authors are experts on their topics.

reliable sources ☑

Who is the author? ☐

Picture two Web sites about the digestive system. One is written by a medical doctor. The site is sponsored by a health organization. The other site was created by someone who isn't in the medical field. Which is probably a better source of information?

How do you find out who the author is? The author may be listed as a specific person or an organization. Check the top and bottom of the Web page. Sometimes the author's name is listed there. Other times, it is on a separate page.

Search the site for the following links: About Us, About this Site, Who are We?, Click to Learn More, Authors, or FAQ.

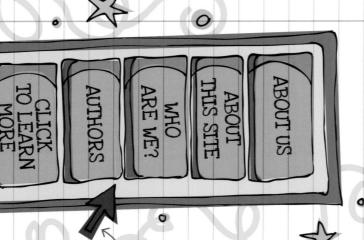

FAQ

CLICK TO LEARN MORE

AUTHORS

WHO ARE WE?

ABOUT THIS SITE

ABOUT US

You may find the information by clicking a button like this on the Web site. Sometimes it is listed as a link at the top or bottom of the page.

14

These links may bring you to pages with information about the author. You can also try returning to the main page and doing some detective work from there.

Pretend you found the author's name. But you have never heard of him or her. Can you find a biography of the author on the Web site? If not, try looking up your author's name using a search engine. You may find more information about the author on a different site. This can help you decide if the author is an expert.

Imagine finding two sites that are both written by experts. But their information does not agree. That may happen from time to time. Take both sides of an idea or conclusion into account. Test them against the rest of your research. Considering different points of view can help you better understand a subject. You may decide to present both sides of the topic.

DID YOU KNOW THIS?

Wikis are Web sites that can be edited by anyone. Not everyone who helps edit a wiki page is an expert. In fact, people might post incorrect information. Many times, you cannot track down information about the people who edit a wiki. For these reasons, many teachers will not let you use wikis for research.

TRY THIS!

Test your skills as a site author investigator. Find a Web site on Christopher Columbus.

1. After you've picked a site, start looking around. Find where the author information is located.

2. Is the author of the Columbus site listed as a person or an organization? Is the author an expert on the topic? How can you tell?

3. Perform a Web search of the author to be sure the person or organization can be trusted to give you expert information. Make your search specific if the author has a common name. You may want to search for the author's first and last name, plus terms such as social studies or history. Can you find any extra information about the author's background or past projects?

Author's Background

Use your findings to make an informed decision. Is the author an expert? Can you trust the person or information that the person or organization provides? You've just used your thinking skills to analyze a site author. You've another step closer to finding the right site!

CHAPTER THREE
Why IS This Web Site Here?

Discovering the purpose of a Web site is important. Remember that sites might want to inform you, persuade you, or sell you something. Knowing the site's purpose can help you decide if it fits your needs. Look for clues that reveal if the site was made for children or adults. Is the text full of difficult vocabulary? The Web site might be written for older readers. Are there many pictures with captions? Is the text large? Do you understand most of the words? The site might be

If a Web site has a lot of big words that you don't understand, it is probably meant for adults. Keep searching for a better site for you!

meant for kids. Sometimes the title of the site states for whom it was meant. Children's sites may have titles that include the word *kids*. Web sites for kids are often more likely to inform you, not persuade you. But you still have to be careful!

Another way to discover the purpose of a site is to look at the URL. A URL is an address. You type the URL into the address line of your browser. You will then get to the exact page you want to see.

Take a close look at the URL to see who might have published the Web site. The publisher is the person or group of people who put the site on the Internet. The publisher may or may not be the same person as the author.

CAUTION TIP:

Be careful about using blogs. Blogs are like online journals. They often contain opinions rather than facts. You might be able to tell if a site is a blog by looking at the URL. Blog URLs often have some form of the word blog in them.

The last three letters of a URL give you some important information about a web site.

URLs that have .com are from businesses. URLs that have .edu are from colleges or schools. An address with .org is from an organization. A URL with .gov is from the government. Sites from museums and government agencies are good choices for school projects. Sites from organizations, schools, and libraries might be smart options, too.

Watch out for personal Web sites. They are less likely to contain expert information. Look closely at the URL. Web sites with words such as *tripod.lycos.com* and *weebly.com* are free sites that anybody can create. So are sites with *homestead.com* and *webs.com*. You will also want to look for a tilde (~) in the URL. This symbol often means that the page is a personal site.

TRY THIS!

Try determining the purpose of three web sites. You can choose sites about Columbus. Or you can practice by using sites about other topics that interest you. You might want to try searching sites for local zoos or museums. Can you figure out the site's purpose? Why does it exist? To inform? To sell something? Some other reason? Keep in mind that some sites have more than one purpose. Many zoos, for example, have sites with facts and pictures about different animals. Zoo sites are often very helpful for projects on wildlife. In that sense, they inform. But do you see any links to information on special events at the zoo? How about ticket sales or specials? Think about it. Could the site also be trying to persuade you to visit the zoo? Remember to keep a site's purpose in mind. It is a smart strategy that will help you decide whether or not a site is right for you.

Many web sites have pictures on them. What can you learn from a picture?

CHAPTER FOUR

Judging a Book Web Site by Its Cover

You've probably heard the expression "Don't judge a book by its cover." It means you shouldn't make up your mind about something based on its appearance alone. When you evaluate a Web site, however, appearances can be important. How a site looks can tell you many things. A site's design can give clues about its purpose and quality. It can also say much about the site's author and publisher. These clues may help you decide if the information is accurate.

Does the Web site look good? Is it neat and organized?

Are the buttons easy to find?

SEARCH

Take a good look when you visit a site. What are your first thoughts about the page? Does it have a nice design? Is the layout organized? Is it colorful? Are there images? Does it seem easy to navigate? You want to be able to find your way around the Web site easily. Web sites that have nice designs often mean that people worked hard on the layout. This may also mean that they or others worked hard to find good information to share.

Consider THIS

Don't be fooled. Attractive Web sites often—but not always—have accurate information. A well-designed site can still have incorrect data. And plain Web sites can have a lot of useful information. The appearance of a Web site is only one thing to consider when finding the right site.

Does the Web site feature a lot of advertisements on the page? Is more space given to those advertisements than to information on the topic? Flashing images on the side or top of a page can be distracting. Many advertisements could also mean that the site was created to sell you something rather than just inform you. To be sure, however, you will have to look closely. You should not automatically ignore a site just because it has some advertisements. Remember to take other clues into account.

Evaluate Web sites carefully. That way you will be sure to use the best ones for your project.

23

TRY THIS!

Choose any site about Christopher Columbus. Can't think of one? Try America's Story from America's Library (www.americaslibrary.gov/cgi-bin/page.cgi). Find the "Search" tab. See if you can find information using "Christopher Columbus" as your search terms. After you find a page on Columbus, take a good look at the site. Does it seem neat and organized? Are there useful images or timelines? Can you easily move from one page to the next or return to the home page? What else do you notice about the design or appearance of the site? Does it look like a lot of thought and time went into presenting the information?

If you are still not sure if you can trust the site after examining its appearance, think about other clues. If you used the America's Story from America's Library site, what can you tell from the URL? Do you see .gov? What does that mean about the site?

URL

CHAPTER FIVE

Putting the Clues Together

The process of Web site evaluation helps you think about the sites you come across in different ways. The clues you gather might tell you who wrote a Web site. They also tell you who published the Web site and why. The goal is to decide if the information is accurate. You want only the best data for your research. Your work is not done after you gather clues. You must put them together. Only then can you decide if you should use the Web site for your research.

Evaluating Web sites can be a bit like solving a puzzle!

Sometimes you cannot find many clues. This may mean that the Web site is not complete. You should find a better option for your research. Other times, clues are misleading. Some Web sites, for example, look great. But they contain incorrect information. This is why it is important to look for many clues, not just one or two.

Considering the clues together can also help you make sure that a Web site truly meets your information needs. Some sites don't answer your research questions. You usually need to use more than one Web site for a research project. That is a smart idea. You can be sure you are getting the best information for your project.

Don't be fooled by a good-looking Web site. Make sure the information is accurate, too!

TRY THIS!

Have you ever seen a detective writing in a notebook while gathering clues? Smart researchers take notes on the clues they find, too. Jot down some observations about the sites you are evaluating. You might use a checklist such as the one on the following page for each site you evaluate. Try to answer each question. Put any notes in the "Your Clues" box. Or put a question mark there if you cannot find that specific information on the site. Then decide if this information puts you in favor of using the site or against using the site.

(continued on page 28)

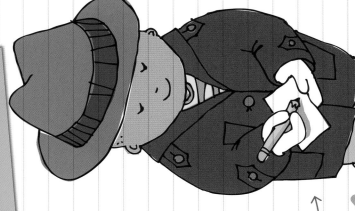

Smart Web site detectives take plenty of notes!

TRY THIS! (CONTINUED)

Put a check mark in the correct box, but don't write in the book! Make a copy of the chart and write on your copy.

Stop! Don't write in the book!

STOP

Gather Clues	Your Clues	In Favor	Against
Does the information make sense?			
Can you verify the information on the site against an expert source or two other web sites?			
Does the site list the date it was created or updated?			
Are there references or links to other sites?			
Is an author or publisher listed?			
Is the author an expert?			
What is the purpose of the site? To sell? Inform? Persuade?			
Another reason?			
What URL clues can you find?			
What design clues do you see? Are there pictures, photographs, or maps?			
Is the site easy to navigate?			
Is the vocabulary on the web site easy for you to read and understand?			
Are there advertisements on the page? Why?			

Now put your clues together. Can you trust the information on the site? Why or why not?

Self-assessment

Good work, Web site detectives! You are well on your way to successful research. Practice the strategies you have learned in this book. Then nothing will get by you. You'll soon become an expert at finding the best online resources for your research.

Finding the right site may not have been easy. But the process has helped improve your evaluation skills. By now, you know that you can't trust everything you find on the Internet. You must analyze Web sites before you use them. Then you can make smart decisions about the quality of a site and its information. Take a moment for some self-assessment. Do you need practice deciding if a site author is an expert on the topic? Could you become better at analyzing the appearance of a page? Thinking about points that you can work on is important. It will help improve your online investigations.

Glossary

accurate **(AK-yuh-ruht)** free of errors or mistakes

bibliography (bib-lee-OG-ruh-fee) a list of writings about a subject or by one author

blogs **(BLAWGZ)** Web sites that have personal, online journals with entries from their authors

navigate **(NAV-uh-gate)** to find one's way around or move through

references **(REF-uh-ren-siz)** sources of information

reliable sources **(ri-LYE-uh-buhl SOR-siz)** well-researched sources of information that are written by experts, have been reviewed by other experts in the field, and are usually current, depending on the topic

search engine **(SURCH EN-juhn)** a tool used to find information on the World Wide Web

self-assessment **(self-uh-SESS-muhnt)** the process of rating your progress, strengths, and weaknesses and determining points that need improvement or changes you can make

Web site evaluation **(WEB SITE i-val-yoo-AY-shuhn)** the process of analyzing a Web site in order to make informed judgments on its accuracy, purpose, and other factors

wikis **(WI-keez)** Web sites that allow users to add and edit content and information

works cited **(WURKSS SYE-tid)** a list of sources from which quotes or information are used in a report or other project

30

Find Out More

BOOKS

Gaines, Ann Graham. *Ace Your Internet Research*. Berkeley
Heights, NJ: Enslow Publishers, 2009.

Hamilton, John. *Internet*. Edina, MN: ABDO Publishing Company,
2005.

Jakubiak, David J. *A Smart Kid's Guide to Doing Internet
Research*. New York: PowerKids Press, 2010.

WEB SITES

Critical Evaluation of a Web Site—Elementary School Level

school.discoveryeducation.com/schrockguide/pdf/evalelem.pdf

Need help determining if a Web site is reliable? Use this guide to
help you.

The Five W's of Web Site Evaluation

kathyschrock.net/abceval/5ws.pdf

Look here for tips on deciding if a Web site is right for your
project.

Web Research Guide—Evaluating a Web Site

*www.classzone.com/books/research_guide/evaluating_web_sites_
guide.pdf*

Find another guide to help you evaluate Web sites.

Index

accuracy, 5, 7, 10,
11–12, 13, 21, 22,
25
addresses. *See URLs*
advertisements, 23
America's Library,
24
authors, 6, 9, 10,
13–16, 18, 21, 25,
29

blogs, 18

checklists, 27–28
current events
research, 9

design, 6, 21–23, 24,
29

encyclopedias, 8, 11,
12
errors, 7
experts, 6, 13, 15,
16, 19, 29

fact-checking, 8,
11–12, 18, 22, 26

Google, 4. *See also*
search engines
.gov sites, 19, 24

history research, 4,
8–9
home pages, 10, 15,
24

informational sites,
6, 9, 17, 18, 20

librarians, 8, 11
libraries, 4, 19, 24
links, 10, 14–15, 20

museums, 19, 20

navigation, 22
notes, 27

.org sites, 19
organization, 22, 24

personal sites, 18,
19
point of view, 6, 9,
15, 18

publishers, 18, 21,
25
purpose, 6, 9, 17–19,
20, 21

references, 10

search engines, 4,
15, 16
search terms, 7, 24
self-assessment, 29

teachers, 8, 11, 15
textbooks, 8
tilde (~), 19
titles, 18
trusted sources, 6, 8,
12, 13, 16

updates, 8–9, 10
URLs, 10, 18–19, 24

vocabulary, 6, 17

Web site evalua-
tion, 5, 12, 21, 25,
27–28, 29
wikis, 15

zoos, 20

About the Author

Ann Truesdell is a school library media specialist and teacher in Michigan. Ann and her husband love to travel and spend time with their son and daughter.